Discover Dartmoor

Paul White

Bossiney Books

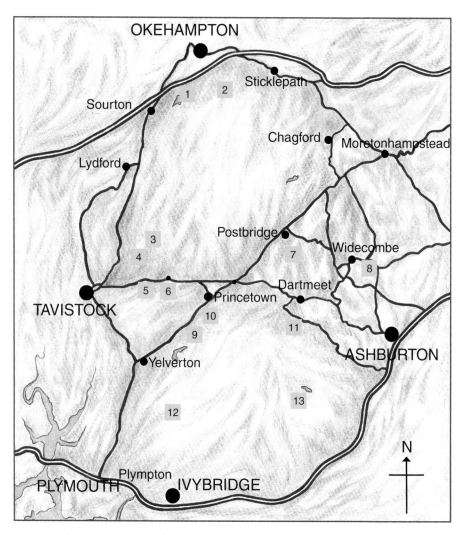

The approximate locations of the walks in the companion book
Really Short Walks to Explore Dartmoor are shown by green squares.

First published 2019 by
Bossiney Books Ltd, 67 West Busk Lane, Otley, LS21 3LY
www.bossineybooks.com

© 2019 Paul White All rights reserved
ISBN 978-1-906474-78-2

Acknowledgements
The maps are by Graham Hallowell. All photographs are by the author.

Printed in Great Britain by R Booth Ltd, Penryn, Cornwall

2

Introduction

Dartmoor is a large area, the National Park alone being 368 square miles (954 km²), and despite its apparent wildness there is much to discover and understand about Dartmoor's history – and its prehistory. How can you best start exploring it?

This book has been organised as four circuits. It is not obligatory to follow them precisely!

If you are short of time, or if a member of your party is not very mobile, you could simply drive round them without leaving your car. However, we have suggested a few short exploratory strolls, mostly just a few hundred metres. For those readers with the time to explore further, another book, *Really Short Walks to Explore Dartmoor*, has been published as a companion to this book.

The starting points for the four circuits are the four 'stannary towns', which in the Middle Ages had the monopoly of trading in tin and were responsible for extracting the tax due to the Duchy of Cornwall or the Crown. Tavistock, Chagford and Ashburton were made stannary towns in 1305, with Plympton joining them in 1328. These towns are well spread out, so they make good starting points wherever you are staying.

If you are short of time and do not expect to drive all four, the Tavistock circuit will give you the best initial understanding of the moor, as well as being the easiest drive. The Plympton circuit is also straightforward, especially if you avoid Sheepstor.

Driving on Dartmoor

If you are not used to country driving, the narrowness of the Dartmoor lanes may come as a shock. Even the 'main' roads crossing the moor, including the A382 which is used by coaches, narrow down to single track in places; the lesser lanes are in many cases single track with passing places. If you are nervous about this, or are not confident reversing, please don't attempt the Chagford or Ashburton circuits.

The very narrowest lanes, which you may well want to avoid, are indicated by the text being printed in blue.

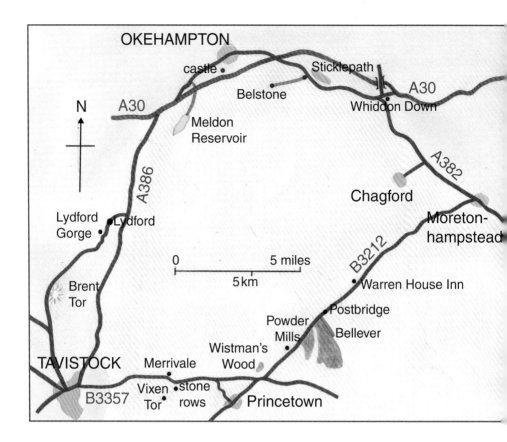

A circuit from Tavistock

This tour is a circuit, but is divided into two parts. The first, from Tavistock to Moretonhampstead, is the route we would recommend to somebody with minimal time to explore Dartmoor – even perhaps returning from a Cornish holiday and taking a diversion on the way to Exeter. The second part, from Moretonhampstead to Okehampton and back to Tavistock, whilst longer in distance, will take less time.

Leave Tavistock by the A386, OKEHAMPTON, and shortly bear right, B3357 PRINCETOWN. After a long climb you will cross a cattle grid, then the road flattens out and you know you're on the moor. To either side of the road you will see the tell-tale signs of former tin-workings.

    Away to the right is the strange shape of Vixen Tor, which is

4

sometimes said to resemble a sphinx. There's a legend that a witch called Vixana once lived there, luring walkers to their doom. Nowadays the landowner keeps all walkers and climbers away from the tor itself.

The road begins to descend to Merrivale, passing on the left first the disused Merrivale quarry then the Dartmoor Inn, before crossing the river Walkham. There is an older bridge to the left, built in the 1770s, when the turnpike road was significantly improved and a still older clapper bridge was replaced.

A little further on lies one of Dartmoor's greatest archaeological treasures, the Merrivale ceremonial complex. Park about 3/4 mile (1.3 km) beyond the bridges, in a car park marked by a rarity in

Tavistock

Tavistock Abbey was founded in AD 981 and the town later developed alongside it, growing fast when tin was discovered on western Dartmoor. It was made a Borough c 1160. By 1600 tin mining had all but ceased and the cloth trade was thriving, then from 1790-1870 copper mining became hugely successful – until it too suddenly collapsed and the town's population decreased. The Russell family, Earls and later Dukes of Bedford, had acquired Tavistock at the Dissolution of the Monasteries and they created the attractive town we see today.

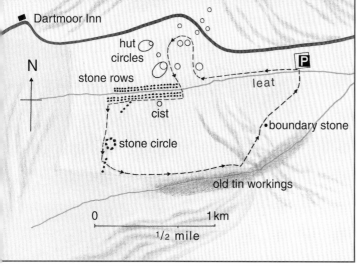

The map suggests the best way to see the Merrivale site (photo opposite) taking in all the stone rows, a stone circle, the ancient settlement, later tin workings and a medieval boundary stone

Merrivale ceremonial complex

This arangement is one the most impressive prehistoric features on Dartmoor, dominated by two double stone rows but also including cairns, a stone circle, a standing stone and a nearby group of hut circles.

this part of Dartmoor – deciduous trees. Go through the gap in the wall at the back of the car park, turn right beside the leat ('leat' is the West Country term for a man-made watercourse) and you will soon see two double stone rows ahead of you.

Now continue towards Princetown. We have included Princetown itself in the tour from Plympton (see page 36) so you can proceed on the B3357 towards TWO BRIDGES.

Diversion. If you prefer to visit Princetown now, turn right at the top of the hill. You will pass the entrance to the prison on your left. The prison has its own museum, and there is a National Park Visitor Centre with free exhibitions situated in the former Duchy Hotel, where Conan Doyle stayed when writing *The Hound of the Baskervilles*. There are numerous cafés and small shops.

At the T-junction turn left on the B3212 past the Railway Inn and Fox Tor Café. this will take you towards Two Bridges. Turn right at the T-junction, B3357 DARTMEET.

If you fancy another interesting short walk (4 km, 2 1/2 miles) to explore Wistman's Wood, park opposite the Two Bridges Hotel.

6

Wistman's Wood

This wood, at 440 m altitude, consists of dwarf oaks and their unique lichens, and it is one of the few vestiges of the primeval woodland of Dartmoor. It was people, of course, who destroyed most of it – but for once the 21st century and global warming are not responsible: the woodland clearances of Dartmoor began 7000 years ago, and the destruction was virtually complete by 2000 BC.

The name Wistman's is a reference to the Devil, who used to lurk near this spot in the form of a huntsman with his hounds, ready to chase sinners into the wood, where the hounds would devour them. 'Wisht' is dialect for 'weird' or 'supernatural'.

The route to Wistman's Wood is fairly straight-forward, as shown on the map. Please don't enter the wood itself as the environment needs to remain undisturbed

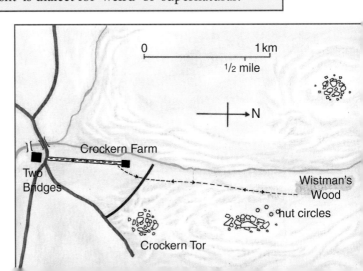

The Stannary Parliament

Crockern Tor was the venue for the Stannary Parliament, an open air meeting of the tinners of Dartmoor (those who owned tin-works, not usually those who got their hands dirty) who had legal rights. They contested the power of the Westminster parliament within the stannaries, and even arrested an MP who objected to them silting up the River Plym. It is said that Sir Walter Raleigh, as Lord Warden of the Stannaries, presided at some of these meetings.

From Two Bridges, continue east and at the junction turn left, B3212 POSTBRIDGE, MORETONHAMPSTEAD. Almost immediately you will pass Crockern Tor, home of the ancient Stannary parliament.

After about 1 3/4 miles (3 km) you will pass on your left the Powder Mills: today it houses a pottery and bunk-house, but it was built in 1844 as a factory for making the gunpowder needed by both quarries and mines. The buildings you can see from the road were for housing the workers, the actual factory being 300 m away as a safety precaution.

You will now start to descend gently towards Postbridge.

Diversion. You may want to take a diversion just before you reach Postbridge, turning right to BELLEVER, where there is a car park (to the left at the T-junction, then signed on the right) within a conifer plantation, giving access to an attractive picnic site beside the river.

Beside the river at Bellever

The Powder Mills

Postbridge is famous for its clapper bridge, which is believed to date from the 13th century, though the first mention of it is in 1380. Each of the slabs across which you can walk weighs more than 8 tonnes. The first use of the name 'Post-Bridge' was in John Ogilby's maps of England's 'post-roads' (tracks along which 'post-boys' carried the mail in their saddle bags), published in 1675:

> At 21.7 [miles from Exeter] cross a stone bridge of 3 arches called Post-Bridge over a brook, and at 23.4 another stone bridge over Cherry Brook.

Forestry

Dartmoor's coniferous forests were mostly planted by the Duchy of Cornwall immediately after WW1, when the demands of trench warfare had all but eliminated the nation's timber reserves. They are now controlled by the Forestry Commission, who are conscious of landscaping, conservation and recreational needs and are trying to increase the proportion of broad-leaved trees – which is a very slow process if you start with more than 90% conifers. Dartmoor's native woodlands, in the Dart valley for example, are mainly oak.

The 'modern' bridge dates from about 1780, when the post-road had become a turnpike, redesigned to take wheeled vehicles – in theory at least.

Continue past the Warren House Inn. (Ogilby's 1675 'road' diverged here and went not through Moretonhampstead but through the then more important town of Chagford.) Just over half a mile (900 m) beyond the Warren House Inn, stop at a parking place beside medieval Bennett's Cross, one of the best places on the moor to see the remnants of tin mining.

Birch Tor and Vitifer mines

This large area has the most substantial evidence of mining on the moor and, being near the road, can be explored – but only with great care,. More than a hundred men worked here, many walking a great distance to work, then sleeping in a shed for their week's labours, but there were cottages too, of which nothing remains. Vitifer was worked by different and increasingly efficient methods in the middle ages and afterwards, then from 1820 to 1870, and then again from 1900 to 1914. As with most of Dartmoor's mines, it was powered by water, here brought by a seven mile leat. Nearby Golden Dagger mine was only finally abandoned in 1939.

A very short stroll downhill to the right here will take you into the area of Birch Tor and Vitifer Mines. Be very cautious, and don't take children or dogs. Among the huge gulleys which you will see there are also shafts, now concealed by vegetation, and accidents occur nearly every year in one old mining region or another.

Diversion. Beyond Bennett's Cross there is another possible diversion, involving a very short but steep walk, to the Bronze Age village of Grimspound. To do this, take the sharp right turn a mile and a quarter (2.2 km) from Bennett's Cross signed WIDECOMBE. After 1 1/2 miles (2.4 km), just before the lane bends to the right, there is parking on the right for half a dozen cars. Walk up the path opposite, which leads to this ancient site.

Retrace your steps to the B3212 and turn right, following the road past the Miniature Pony Centre to Moretonhampstead, an attractive little town despite having lost many of its old buildings to fires. If in a hurry, bypass the town by turning left before you get to the centre. Otherwise head to the centre and take the A382 to the left. See page 22 for further information about Moretonhampstead.

The second half of this tour is deliberately simple. If you are in a hurry, just join the A30 at Whiddon Down, bypass Okehampton and turn left on the A386 towards Tavistock. You can stay on the A386 instead of going via Lydford.

On the other hand, if you have time to spare, some of the villages you will pass between Whiddon Down and Okehampton are covered in more detail in the Chagford circuit (pages 17-20).

The A382 goes to Whiddon Down. On reaching a mini-roundabout, turn left, STICKLEPATH. This road was the A30 before the dual carriageway was built. It curves around the mediaeval township of South Zeal, then goes through the village of Sticklepath.

Beyond Sticklepath cross over the A30 to visit Okehampton, which is home to the Museum of Dartmoor Life as well as the ruins of an 11th century castle (English Heritage). Even if you don't intend to visit the castle, it's worth passing it. To do so, turn left at the traffic lights in the town centre (GEORGE STREET, immediately before the White Hart Hotel) and take the second right, CASTLE ROAD, which crosses a bridge, then passes the castle and rejoins the old main road. Keep left at a junction.

Okehampton Castle

The Highwayman at Sourton

Diversion. Immediately before you join the modern A30, there is a possible diversion to Meldon Reservoir, which was built as recently as 1972 and was controversial at the time. Simply cross the dual carriageway (begun in 1986 and also controversial for cutting through the National Park) and follow signs to the reservoir car park. There are attractive walks across the reservoir dam and beside the water, or down towards the impressive former railway viaduct.

Otherwise, take the A30 towards LAUNCESTON but leave it at the first exit, A386 TAVISTOCK. At Sourton this passes the bizarre Highwayman Inn, directly opposite which is a Romano-Christian inscribed stone, later used as a waymark cross. Just before reaching the Dartmoor Inn, turn right to LYDFORD.

Once through Lydford and beyond the entrance to Lydford Gorge, the road continues south to pass Brent Tor, which some 350 million years ago was an active volcano.

There is a small 13th century church on the top, inevitably dedicated to St Michael and equally inevitably with a legend that the Devil unsuccessfully tried to prevent its construction. There is a car park at its foot, should you feel like a climb to a viewpoint.

From Brent Tor, simply follow signs to Tavistock.

Lydford and Lydford Gorge

King Alfred established Lydford as one of four Devon 'burhs', fortified towns, and it is said to have repulsed a Viking raid in 997. It was a much more important place than its present appearance suggests, with its own mint, and was apparently the second most populous place in Devon. However, since Lydford parish was at that time enormous, incorporating the whole of Dartmoor, perhaps the 'town' itself was not that large. Under the Normans the castle became an administrative centre and served as the stannary prison – a place not famed for justice.

> I oft have heard of Lydford law,
> How in the morn they hang and draw,
> And sit in judgement after.

The church is famous for the amusing epitaph of George Routledge, watch-maker, which is now found inside the church.

Lydford Gorge (National Trust) has both a magnificent waterfall and 'the Devil's Cauldron'. The walk can be thoroughly recommended – though it's quite strenuous.

A circuit from Chagford

This circuit can easily be divided into two parts. The first encompasses a number of attractive villages (you may well want to stroll around some of them) and ancient farmhouses. If you are interested in vernacular architecture, this is the route for you!

The north-eastern side of Dartmoor has more moderate rainfall than the western side, and is sheltered by the moor, which probably

---

Chagford

Chagford itself now feels like a large village, but historically it was a stannary town and its centre is largely unspoilt, much of it sixteenth or seventeenth century, with white rendering and thatch. The Three Crowns opposite the church is particularly imposing, and was a gentry house before it became an inn.

There are two stories of fatal shootings in Chagford. In 1641 Mary Whiddon was murdered by a jealous suitor as she came out of the church on her wedding day – an incident which RD Blackmore transported to Exmoor and used in the plot of *Lorna Doone*. And two years later, during a Civil War skirmish, a Cavalier officer, Sydney Godolphin, was shot in the porch of Whiddon House, which has now become the Three Crowns.

Apparently both their ghosts still haunt the inn...

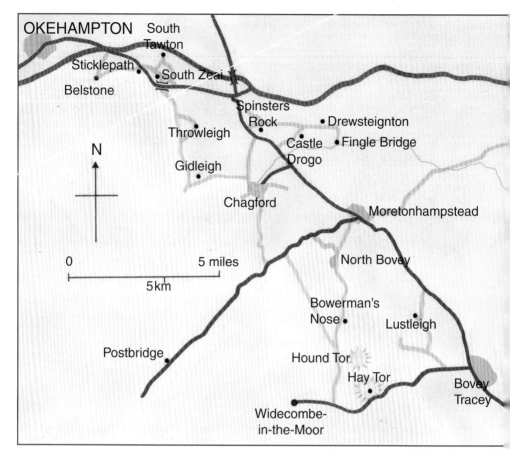

accounts for its historically slightly denser population. There
is more farmland, as well as areas of deciduous woodland. The
second part of the circuit includes both delightful villages and
moorland.

Warning: in this circuit there are a number of narrow single
track lanes with passing places.

Facing uphill in Chagford's main square, turn right. At a fork,
bear right down a narrow lane. Keep right to cross the River Teign
and take the first left, MURCHINGTON. Go through the hamlet
of Murchington and then to Gidleigh. Continue past the sign
GIDLEIGH, CHAPPLE (which leads to Gidleigh Castle, a small tower
house, visible from the lane but with no access) till you reach a
junction.

Throwleigh

Diversion. For one of the most evocative short walks on Dartmoor, including a stone circle and several stone rows, continue ahead, SCORHILL, to a small car park. See *Fairly Easy Walks on Dartmoor*, Walk 3, for details.

Alternatively, turn right, CREABER. Ignore side turnings and before long you will cross a cattle-grid and begin to follow the edge of the open moor. Continue till you reach a right turn signed THROWLEIGH. This is a very pretty village, but approached by a narrow lane: you could avoid this by continuing ahead, SOUTH ZEAL.

Take the lane to Throwleigh and you will pass Shilstone Farm, a 15th century longhouse with 16th and 17th century additions. Pevsner says it is 'perhaps the most architecturally distinguished of all surviving longhouses', though it's hard to appreciate it fully when driving past. In Throwleigh turn left at the church and head for SOUTH ZEAL.

Entering South Zeal, bear left into the 30 mph zone and go under a bridge. Descend the lane to a T-junction, and turn left. You are now in the main street of the village, which was, from 1760 until 1829 when the first bypass was built, the main road from Exeter to Okehampton. It takes you past the Oxenham Arms, then a chapel in the former market place, and then the Kings Arms.

South Zeal

The main street (photo above) was once the main Exeter to Okehampton road, and the village was created in the 13th century to try to exploit that. It was never a great success, which means that the early layout survives surprisingly intact. The houses each have a street frontage and a 'burgage plot' and the plots appear to have been a furlong in length (220 yards, 201m).

Turn left at a crossroads (FORD CROSS, OKEHAMPTON) then right when you reach the main road, which will take you into Sticklepath (photo below). 'Stickle' is an old word meaning steep and difficult.

On the left as you go through the village is Finch Foundry, a nineteenth century water-powered forge which made metal tools and is now maintained by the National Trust. There are frequent demonstrations of its machinery.

A walk. If you fancy a short walk (2.5 km/1 ½ miles) through Skaigh Woods, walk down the main street to the bridge and turn right (PUBLIC BRIDLEPATH). Stay the same side of the river, go through a gate, then turn right. Follow the path beside the river to a foot-bridge, then return along the far side by track and then lane. While most of the walk is easy, in a couple of places there are tricky rocks to negotiate, and it can be muddy.

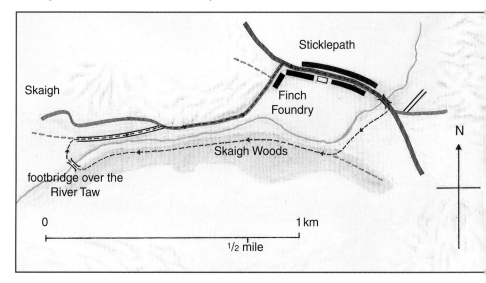

You now have choices – whether to divert to the villages of Belstone and/or South Tawton, or simply to turn round and head back along the B 3260 towards Whiddon Down.

South Tawton is distinctive for its attractive and quaint build-ings, Belstone for its situation, its village green, village stocks and places of refreshment. There is also a small cairn circle 1 km walk from the village centre, see *Really Short Walks to Explore Dartmoor,* Walk 2.

To visit Belstone, turn left, SKAIGH, at the far end of the Sticklepath village street. (The tarmac footpath uphill to your right was the old

19

main road – the original steep and muddy 'stickle path'.) After a dog-leg at Skaigh the lane leads to Belstone.

Take a turn round the triangular village green but instead of returning via Skaigh, bear left, OKEHAMPTON, passing the village car park. On reaching the B3260, turn right and go back through Sticklepath but immediately after the river bridge (over the infant River Taw) bear left, unsigned.

At a crossroads, turn left, SOUTH TAWTON. From the church and thatched church house, return the same way. Go straight ahead at the crossroads at the top of South Zeal, then turn left, WHIDDON DOWN, EXETER.

At the mini-roundabout at Whiddon Down turn right on A382, MORETONHAMPSTEAD. Then bear left, DREWSTEIGNTON.

Diversion. Alternatively, to visit Dartmoor's oldest structure, Spinster's Rock, continue towards Moretonhampstead. After 1.3 miles (2 km) turn left at a crossroads on a bend into a *very* minor road, SPINSTERS ROCK. After 0.4 miles (700 m) you will find a parking area on the right, opposite farm buildings, and a signpost beside a kissing gate. Continue past Spinster's Rock to a T-junction and turn right, DREWSTEIGNTON, FINGLE BRIDGE.

Spinster's Rock

This is a Neolithic burial chamber, one of Devon's oldest prehistoric monuments, though it collapsed in 1862 and was re-erected. It was probably intended to commemorate a whole community, and not just a prominent individual.

You're aiming for Fingle Bridge, but Drewsteignton is just 100 m off the route and it's well worth the diversion. Then continue to

Drewsteignton and Castle Drogo

The manor was owned in the late 12th century by a certain Drew de Teignton. This did not stop 18th century antiquaries from declaring that the name implied Druids – who of course they believed had constructed Spinster's Rock. 'Drew' was for some reason latinised as Drogo.

Julius Drew (later Drewe), the wealthy founder of the Home & Colonial Stores, Britain's first major grocery retail chain, was convinced by a dodgy genealogist that he was descended from Drew de Teignton (as well as various royalty) which inspired him to buy the estate in 1910, for which he had Edward Lutyens design Castle Drogo.

Building started in 1911 and it was completed in 1930 – the last castle to be built in England. It is now a National Trust property and well worth visiting.

Fingle Bridge. This is a 17th century bridge which once carried considerable packhorse traffic. There is a splendid walk along the Teign westward from the bridge, as well as a riverside pub.

Return past Drewsteignton and bear left to pass Castle Drogo. When you reach the A382 turn left towards Moretonhampstead.

At Moretonhampstead there is a car park just beyond the central crossroads. If you walk back to the crossroads and take the right

Moretonhampstead. The almshouses have a datestone 1637, but were almost certainly built much earlier

22

Lustleigh. You will probably wish to explore the centre of the village on foot

turn towards Dunsford, you will reach the most interesting building in the town, a row of almshouses. Several fires in the early 20th century, particularly in 1926, destroyed many of the town's other old buildings.

Continue south-east from Moretonhampstead for 3 1/2 miles (5.9 km) on the A 382, then turn right, LUSTLEIGH.

Leave by the lane heading south, downhill, RUDGE. Ignore side turnings. At a junction turn left, BOVEY TRACEY, MANATON. Then at a T-junction turn right and cross the River Bovey. At the next T-junction turn left (BOVEY TRACEY) then keep right into a minor road, HAYTOR. This leads to a junction with the B 3387 – which by this stage will appear to you as a major road! Turn right. It will take you to Haytor (photo below).

Haytor

This is one of Dartmoor's largest tors, with dramatic and varied views from its summit. Because it is close to the Torbay resorts it has been popular with excursionists for the last two centuries. High quality granite was quarried in the area from 1820 to 1919, and carried down to the Stover Canal by a tramway – itself consisting of rails carved from granite. A network of these tramway tracks still survives.

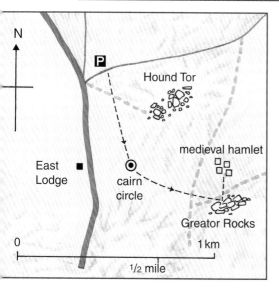

After Haytor the road rises. Take the first turning to the right, HOUND TOR, MANATON. Keep right at the first fork, then right again at the next fork to the car park.

A very short stroll will take you to a medieval hamlet, abandoned shortly before the Black Death, as well as remarkable scenery – see the map.

Below: Hound Tor

From here you have three options, of varying difficulty. For all of them on leaving the car park, turn right, then sharp right at the fork, M'HAMPSTEAD, CHAGFORD.

The first option is to cut the tour short and head directly for Chagford.

The second option is to start on the road towards Chagford. After 1.4 miles (2.2km) turn right (unsigned) and after a further mile (1.6km) turn left and follow signs to the delightful village of NORTH BOVEY.

The third option takes you to the extraordinary rock formation called Bowerman's Nose (see front cover) and then to North Bovey, **but be warned:** the road is very narrow, gated, and when I last drove this way it had many potholes. It might be more sensible to walk to Bowerman's Nose from the Hound Tor car park.

For this route, take the fork signed 'Unsuitable for wide vehicles'. A little way beyond the first gate you will see Bowerman's Nose on the slope of a hillside to your right. At a T-junction, turn left, then at the next junction turn right and follow signs to NORTH BOVEY.

Just as you enter this attractive village, well worth exploring on foot and with a historic pub, there is a car park on the right.

Leave the village heading north on the M'HAMPSTEAD, POSTBRIDGE road. At a junction keep right, M'HAMPSTEAD, POSTBRIDGE, then at a crossroads turn left, POSTBRIDGE, which will bring you to the B3212. Turn left. After 1¹/4 miles (2km) pass the Miniature Pony Centre then take the first right, CHAGFORD. Ignore side turnings and when you arrive at a T-junction by the church, turn left for the square, or right to get to the village car park.

North Bovey

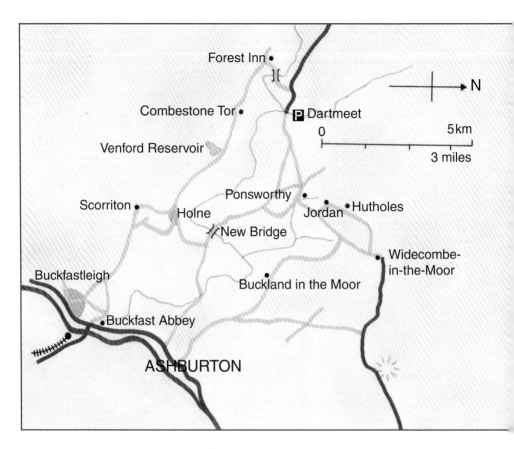

A circuit from Ashburton

Warning: in this circuit there are a number of single track lanes with passing places.

Leave Ashburton on the B3325, and then along the minor road parallel to the A38 towards Buckfastleigh.

At a T-junction turn right, then at a mini-roundabout, turn right again, BUCKFASTLEIGH. This will lead you past Buckfast Carpets, in what was until 2013 an active wool production unit.

Just beyond it is the entrance to Buckfast Abbey. To visit the abbey, after turning left at the mini roundabout turn right into the abbey car park.

Buckfastleigh itself is well worth seeing – a medieval mill town, though largely rebuilt, and we suggest you at least do a quick drive through it. Turn right out of the abbey car park, up the hill and past

Buckfast Abbey and Buckfastleigh

Buckfast is an active Benedictine abbey, re-founded by French Benedictine monks at the end of the 19th century on the site of an earlier abbey, and self-supporting through its farm and the shops on the site, so that it is now a visitor attraction.

In the Middle Ages there was a Cistercian Abbey here, as also at Buckland on the other side of the moor. The Cistercians on Dartmoor, like those in Yorkshire, were active sheep farmers and created a significant woollen industry.

The town of Buckfastleigh developed in the Middle Ages as a mill town, as did neighbouring Ashburton. Paper-making and tanning were important industries here but the core business was woollen manufacture, which continued at the Buckfast Spinning Mill until 2013.

Just outside the town centre lies the headquarters of the South Devon Railway, which runs steam trains to Totnes – a delightful ride – as well as a butterfly farm and otter sanctuary. The town itself remains surprisingly unaffected by the local tourism, retaining its medieval layout though most of the shops and houses are later rebuilds.

the turn on the right to HOLNE which you will take later. Proceed down the hill, past Hamlyn House (the Hamlyn family were mill owners) to a T-junction. Turn left along an older street and keep left at the next junction into narrow Fore Street, which feels quite medieval, though most of the buildings are later – rebuilding being a sign of the town's prosperity.

The Valiant Soldier on the left is a former pub, its interior preserved as a museum of pub life as it was in the 1950s.

Keep left again, cross a stream, then turn left at a T-junction. You will pass on your right two visitor attractions, the South Devon Railway (steam trains to Totnes) and the Butterfly Farm and Otter Sanctuary. Continue to the mini-roundabout and turn left, retracing your previous route.

This time turn right at the top of the hill, HOLNE, SCORRITON. Follow signs to Holne, a pretty village, the birthplace of Charles Kingsley, the muscular Christian, novelist and social reformer. At a T-junction, turn left, HEXWORTHY. Ignore side turnings.

There is parking just beyond the dam at Venford Reservoir (photo above) and there are good walks from here. There is a path right round the reservoir.

A mile or so (1.6km) beyond the reservoir you will pass Combestone Tor (photo above). Stop here and take a look over the Dart Valley, and see if you can make out a pattern of old field boundaries ('reaves') on the opposite side. It's easier in evening light, as they are only a foot or so, perhaps 30-40cm, tall and probably originally had bushes planted down the middle to form a hedge. There are some right next to Combestone Tor, so you can see their structure.

They're very well laid out, at perfect right angles, in a system extending over miles of hilly land, and you might think they're the result of 18th century agricultural enclosure. And they are indeed 18th century, but from the 18th century BC, the early Bronze Age. No less than 407km (253 miles) of these reaves survive on the moor. Our remote ancestors were very ingenious and well organised folk!

After a further mile, keep right to descend steeply. Pass the Forest Inn, then cross Hexworthy Bridge a.k.a. Huccaby Bridge – which *is* 18th century AD! – over the West Dart. The road climbs to meet the Tavistock-Ashburton road. Turn right, passing the quirky Pixieland – a shop which sells a range of sheepskin products and eatables, as well as garden gnomes: the gnomes have their own garden in which you are invited to wander without charge – selfie country.

The remains of a clapper bridge at Dartmeet

Descend again to cross the East Dart, and immediately turn left into the large car park. This is Dartmeet – the East and West Dart rivers converge 50 m below the bridge. There are public toilets, and beyond the car park is the Badgers Holt Tearooms and Restaurant.

The road continues towards Ashburton up a very steep hill. Be glad you're not carrying a coffin up it: people from this area used to have to carry their dead to Widecombe for burial, and part way up the hill the old route has a 'coffin stone', on which the coffin could be placed while the bearers had a brief rest.

Ponsworthy

When the road levels out, bear left at a fork onto a minor road. Ignore side turnings and it will take you down to Ponsworthy. Turn left, WIDECOMBE. You can go straight to Widecombe if in a hurry, or wanting to avoid a very narrow lane.

Diversion. This goes first to Jordan Manor, an early 17th century longhouse in origin though with later improvements, and then to a medieval hamlet called Hutholes.

Hutholes

Hutholes is one of two Dartmoor sites with ruins of medieval longhouses. (The other, Houndtor, see page 24, is in a more evocative setting, but further from a road.) Walk back down the lane, then turn right through a gate as signed.

There are three longhouses and several smaller buildings. The traditional moorland longhouse was divided into two rooms with a cross-passage between them. It was built on a slope, the upper room being the family's only living and sleeping space, and the lower room a cow-shed. The Hutholes group was flourishing in the thirteenth century, but had probably been abandoned before the Black Death.

Widecombe-in-the-Moor

This small village within a large parish is dominated by its substantial parish church, the 'cathedral of the moor'. These days tourism is extremely important to the village economy. The famous annual fair occurs on the second Tuesday of September, when the roads surrounding the village are closed to normal traffic, and park-and-ride services (not cheap) are provided.

After Ponsworthy, take the first lane on the left, which will take you past Jordan, then past Dockwell Farm with its barns. When you see a row of stones stopping you parking on the right, park on the left as soon as convenient in order to visit Hutholes.

Now continue over a crossroads, then turn left at a T-junction into Widecombe.

From Widecombe, you could return to Ashburton by way of Buckland-in-the-Moor, 'one of Dartmoor's dream villages' according to multiple websites, but you might prefer to see a bit of open moor. Leave Widecombe by the B3387 and climb steeply. Take the first right turn and follow signs to ASHBURTON.

Once in Ashburton, cross the River Ashburn and turn right along North Street to the town centre.

A circuit from Plympton

Plympton St Maurice is a gem hidden in the outer suburbs of Plymouth. Its narrow Fore Street in particular has houses with 17th and 18th century frontages – but in many cases the house itself is very much older. Behind them in a park lies a motte and bailey castle, of which little remains except the mound.

The town was laid out as a planned castle town around 1080, with an Augustinian priory added in 1121. In the Middle Ages Plympton was far more important than Plymouth, becoming a stannary town in 1328.

Drive eastward along Fore Street, then turn left up George Lane. On your right is the former grammar school, where the artist Sir Joshua Reynolds received lessons from his father – its Master. Turn left at 'The George' onto Ridgeway, then turn right at a mini-roundabout into MOORLAND ROAD.

At a T-junction by the 'Lord Louis', turn right, then at the next roundabout left. Follow signs to LEE MOOR. At a T-junction, turn sharp left, WOTTER.

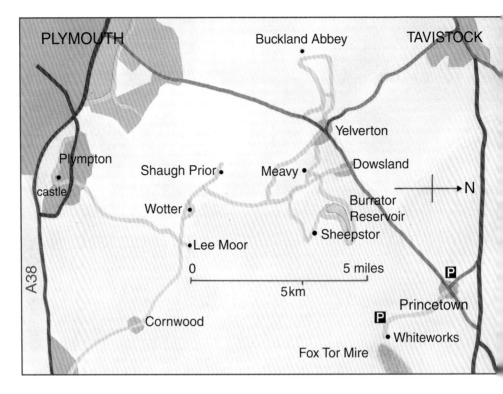

Pass Wotter on your right. In the former china clay works just 100 m north of the village there are in fact two ancient stone rows, each leading up to a cairn, but they are not among Dartmoor's best preserved antiquities. It is amazing that they have survived at all. The former china clay works was delightfully named Wotterwaste.

Half a mile (800 m) beyond Wotter turn right, YELVERTON, TAVISTOCK. You will pass Cadover Bridge, a popular recreational site. The Plym River is particularly attractive here.

Really Short Walks to Explore Dartmoor Walk 12 starts near here, exploring both china clay extraction and prehistoric remains.

Diversion. To avoid narrow lanes, continue to YELVERTON, then turn right towards Princetown.

Otherwise, beyond Cadover Bridge take a minor road to the right, SHEEPSTOR. Take the second turning on the right, SHEEPSTOR, then keep right at a fork. At a T-junction, turn left for Sheepstor.

(There are some fine stone rows at Drizzlecombe, accessed on foot from Nattor. See Walk 11 in *Shortish Walks on Dartmoor*.)

34

China clay country

The area was deliberately excluded from the Dartmoor National Park. China clay, or kaolin, is formed when a certain kind of granite breaks down – a natural process. It is used in many ways, from whitening bathroom fittings to whitening toothpaste, but more than 80% of Dartmoor's china clay goes to make coated paper, as used for this book. It was first quarried here in 1830, though it had been discovered in Cornwall (by a Devonian, William Cookworthy of Kingsbridge) in 1746.

Extraction industries are never pretty, and Dartmoor's china clay country is no exception. It serves as a reminder that parts of the moor were for centuries affected by tin mining or granite quarries – but it should also be remembered that these industries were crucial in giving employment to a significant part of the population in the days before tourism, and that their products were used nationally and internationally – which is still true of china clay.

At present 88% of the UK's china clay is exported (though we then re-import coated paper) but Brazil and China both produce more china clay than does the UK.

Sheepstor church is worth exploring, on account of the strange story of the White Rajahs of Sarawak.

Sheepstor and the White Rajahs

James Brooke (1803-1868) was a soldier and adventurer born in India. He greatly assisted the Sultan of Brunei, who made him first governor, then Rajah, of Sarawak, a title later passed to a nephew and great-nephew, all three of whom are buried at St Leonard's, Sheepstor.

The Brookes were strong rulers in a hugely divided nation, attempting to curb piracy and head-hunting, and they attracted both supporters and enemies – as well as wealth. James Brooke is quoted as saying: 'Sarawak belongs to the Malays, the Sea Dayaks, the Land Dayaks, the Kayans and other tribes, not to us. It is for them that we labour, not ourselves.' Fine words…

Burrator Reservoir

Completed in 1898 and enlarged in 1929, the reservoir holds 4.6 billion litres and was built to serve Plymouth by trapping the River Meavy. The conifers around it were planted in the strange expectation that they would attract rainfall. Whilst its appearance is far from natural for Dartmoor, it is widely appreciated.

Continuing beyond the church you will reach Burrator Reservoir. Cross the dam. If you want to make a circuit of the reservoir, and perhaps visit Burrator Arboretum and Nature Reserve, turn right. Keep turning right, until you cross the dam again.

Princetown

On Benjamin Donn's detailed map of Devon published in 1765, there is no sign of habitation at or near Princetown. It was the creation of one man, Sir Thomas Tyrwhitt (1762-1833), a friend of, and agent for, the Prince of Wales. He built a house at Tor Royal probably in 1798 (though some say a few years earlier) and planned to 'improve' Dartmoor's agriculture.

Both the prison, originally for American prisoners of war in 1812, and the Plymouth & Dartmoor Railway, the trackbed of which still exists and makes a good walk, were his idea. The village economy has had its ups and downs over the years, but its position at the centre of the moor brings it many tourists in the season.

Fox Tor Mire, the original of Conan Doyle's Great Grimpen Mire – a place of desolation

This time turn left, and on reaching a T-junction turn right, DOUSLAND. Reaching the B3212, turn right and head up towards PRINCETOWN and the open moor.

At Princetown you will probably want to park in the village, in which case turn left at the mini-roundabout for the car park. Princetown has numerous places to eat, as well as small shops and the Dartmoor Visitor Centre. The prison also has its own museum.

A walk. There is an enjoyable flat walk to be had along a former railway. Turn left out of the car park along a no-through-road past the fire station, then turn left again on a well surfaced path which soon heads out onto the open moor, leading to quarries.

A diversion to the 'Great Grimpen Mire'

At the T-junction in the centre of Princetown, take the the B3212 past the Railway Inn and Fox Tor Café, then almost immediately turn right into Tor Royal Lane. Follow this for 3 miles (5km) towards the ruins of the former mining hamlet of Whiteworks. There is no parking among the ruins of the hamlet, so park where the lane takes a sharp turn to the left, and walk down, crossing a leat. To your right lies Fox Tor Mire, here described in *Hound of the Baskervilles*:

> We left her standing upon the thin peninsula of firm, peaty soil which tapered out into the widespread bog. From the end of it a small wand planted here and there showed where the path zig-zagged from tuft to tuft of rushes among those green scummed pits and foul quagmires which barred the

The Royal Oak at Meavy

way to the stranger. Rank reeds and lush, slimy water-plants sent an odour of decay and a heavy miasmatic vapour into our faces, while a false step plunged us more than once thigh-deep into the dark, quivering mire, which shook for yards in soft undulations around our feet.

Perhaps a bit exaggerated, but exploration of the mire on foot is not recommended, though there are other good walks in the area – see *Fairly Easy Walks on Dartmoor*, Walk 8 and *Shortish Walks on Dartmoor*, Walk 10.

Return to Princetown and turn left on the B3212, retracing your route.

At Dousland turn left at the cross-roads and head for Meavy. After 3/4 mile (1.3km) turn right into the village of Meavy, where the Royal Oak pub is beautifully situated above the village green. The oak tree itself is thought to be 900 years old, and the hollow in its trunk is said to have been used by the publican in the past as a peat store.

From Meavy continue to Yelverton, turning right at a T-junction into the village; then turn left onto the A386 back towards Plymouth.

However, you are not far from one of the National Trust's most interesting properties, Buckland Abbey, once home of Sir Francis Drake: it's not strictly Dartmoor but you might want to head there...

Ponies

You will not go far on Dartmoor before you see ponies. Everyone agrees they are cute. The traditional Dartmoor pony was both strong and hardy, and although they lived an apparently wild life, they were each year herded up and sold. Once 'broken' they were used on the moor to haul carts or act as packhorses, but many were sold to work undergound in coal mines in South Wales.

When the mines no longer needed them, they were bred for their meat, used in pet food. But now that trade has declined, so they are mostly sold as children's ponies. Since other breeds are apparently even cuter than Dartmoors, most ponies you will see on the moor now are cross-breeds. Please do not feed them, as it encourages them to stay near the roads, where too many get struck. And be aware that they are unbroken: they may well kick or bite.

What have we missed?

Inevitably, a lot!

Perhaps the greatest omission is the high and wild area south of Okehampton, which you can reach by car. From Okehampton follow signs for OKEHAMPTON CAMP. Keep to the left when you reach it, cross a cattle grid and a stream and continue climbing the tarmac road till you reach a large parking area on the right at a fork in the road (SX 596922). This car park is near a military training area. There are good walks from here: sometimes the area is closed off for live firing, but usually not in the tourist season or at weekends.

The army has used the moor for training for more than 200 years.

Other Bossiney books about Dartmoor

Ancient Dartmoor
Dartmoor's History
Really Short Walks to Explore Dartmoor (3-6 km)
Fairly Easy Walks on Dartmoor (3-9 km)
Shortish Walks on Dartmoor (6-8 km)
Dartmoor Pub Walks (7-14 km)
Walks on High Dartmoor (7-20 km)